The Work of the Worship Committee

Linda Bonn

Judson Press® Valley Forge

The Work of the Worship Committee
© 1998 by Judson Press, Valley Forge, PA 19482-0851
All rights reserved.

Library of Congress Cataloging-in-Publication Data
Bonn, Linda.
   The work of the worship committee / Linda Bonn.
p. cm.
ISBN 0-8170-1294-X (pbk. : alk. paper)
1. Worship. 2. Church committees. I. Title.
BV10.2.B76 1998
264—dc21   98-25913

Printed in the U.S.A.
10 09 08 07 06 05 04 03 02 01 00 99 98
5 4 3 2 1

Contents

Preface

"O come, let us worship and bow down . . ."
Psalm 95:6

Martin Luther wrote that "the chief end of humankind is to glorify God and enjoy God forever." Worship committees assist in creating an environment and atmosphere where worship may occur. The act of worship is initiated by God, who calls us to worship, and it is in worship that we respond in adoration and praise, in prayer and proclamation, and in response to the challenge to be renewed for ministry and mission in our community and the world.

As we approach the new millennium, it is no secret that the worshiping church is in crisis. Preaching and music styles are fodder for emotionally charged discussions as congregations struggle to discern their emerging worship identity. The struggles are not only generational or cultural—they relate to differences in education, environment, experience, and expectation among members of the congregation.

It is not only the perspectives of individual worshipers that vary. In any given denomination, one church will differ from another in theology, style, size, culture, and ethnicity. The work of the worship committee reflects its congregation's unique worship identity and values, as well as its polity and structure. This book is not designed to be a set formula for organizing the committee's work; rather, it is an opportunity for pastors, worship committees, and congregations to seek the mind of Christ as they re-examine what makes the content and form of their corporate worship unique and how the worship committee can best realize this integral ministry.

—*Linda Bonn*
Ash Wednesday, 1998

Introduction

We all have a need to reach out beyond ourselves, to acknowledge a higher power in the universe. This acknowledgment of the creative and redemptive powers of the One we call God can grow into an appreciation for God's sovereignty and greatness, and that appreciation can grow further into adoration and love. This acknowledgment, appreciation, and adoration become the basis for what we call "worship."

The word *worship* is derived from the Anglo-Saxon form of "worth" and "ship," meaning "worthiness." As the sovereign power in the universe, God is worthy to be worshiped, and it is God whom we worship. The worthiness of God is recorded throughout Scripture. In Psalm 68:32-35 we read:

Sing to God, O kingdoms of the earth;
    sing praises to the Lord,

O rider in the heavens, the ancient heavens;
　　listen, he sends out his voice, his mighty voice.
Ascribe power to God,
　　whose majesty is over Israel;
　　and whose power is in the skies.
Awesome is God in his sanctuary,
　　the God of Israel;
　　he gives power and strength to his people.
Blessed be God!

Psalm 86:8-10 speaks to the worthiness of God with a sense of adoration and appreciation:

There is none like you among the gods, O Lord,
　　nor are there any works like yours.
All the nations you have made shall come
　　and bow down before you, O Lord,
　　and shall glorify your name.
For you are great and do wondrous things;
　　you alone are God.

Worship begins with God. It is God who calls us to worship, and it is in worship that we respond to God's ongoing revelation. God, in service to humankind, reveals Godself to us in the person of Jesus Christ, and we, in service to God, respond, performing for God's pleasure, giving glory to the One who is worthy of all our praise. We become, as Sören Kierkegaard noted, "the actors." God is the "audience," and the worship leaders are the "prompters." The service of worship becomes a time for all God's people, laity and clergy together, to participate in this divine drama.

When we worship God, we reach beyond ourselves to experience life at a new level of consciousness. The routines of life are put aside for the moment, and, as James White states in *New Forms of Worship,* "we come to approach all of life in a greater sense of depth than our normal consciousness allows opportunity for."

The act of worship is a celebration. It is said that "we celebrate or die." When Christians come together around the Word, font, and table, we enter into praise, prayer, proclamation, and remembrance. We proclaim the mystery of our faith—that Christ has died, Christ has risen, Christ will come again. We remember the acts of salvation history, give thanks for the victory of Christ's resurrection, and anticipate the promise of Christ's coming again in glory.

The role of the Holy Spirit in worship is paramount. The Spirit validates the cultic expression "Jesus Christ is Lord," for only by the Spirit's power can this statement be truthfully made (1 Corinthians 12:3). The Spirit also sets the stage for transformation by bringing believers together in a mystical alliance as we center on worshiping Christ as Head of the Church. The Spirit does this by creating an atmosphere that helps worshipers praise God, trust God for life itself, and trust each other in the spiritual union that is the body of Christ. The Spirit serves as the worshipers' guide—empowering, convicting, illuminating, and renewing. Having laypersons fully participate in the planning and leading of worship is as old as the Judeo-Christian tradition. Old Testament worship reflected the idea of the unity between people and priests. Worship was intentional action, involving not only the mind and spirit, but also the body. Psalm 95:1, 2, and 6 read:

> O come, let us sing to the LORD;
>> let us make a joyful noise to the rock of our salvation!
> Let us come into his presence with thanksgiving;
>> let us make a joyful noise to him with songs of praise!
> O come, let us worship and bow down,
>> let us kneel before the LORD, our Maker!

Reading the energetic cadence of this scripture provides us with the image of vibrant and living worship, with everyone actively participating. In the temple, people sang, played musical instruments, and wrote psalms that would become the basis of biblical praise and thanksgiving in today's worship. Many of the psalms were written in parallel style, suggesting antiphonal chanting during the service.

From the time of the Babylonian exile, worship in the synagogue was highly participatory in nature. In fact, the word *synagogue* means "congregation." The chief officer of the synagogue was the *ruler,* chosen from the congregation because of his moral and spiritual virtues. He presided over the assembly and chose the prophetic lesson. The *servant* of the synagogue handled the detailed arrangement of services and administration. The *messenger* was selected from the people to lead in the recitation or pray on the congregation's behalf. The *Herald of the Shema* read from the scroll or led an antiphonal recitation from it. This style continued in the New Testament. In Luke 4:16-20, Jesus enters the synagogue and participates in worship by reading from the prophet Isaiah. Prayers were recited antiphonally, or a member of the congregation would lead in intercessory prayer, followed by a congregational "Amen." The sermon or homily was given by any person in the assembly who was considered "suitable" or by visitors, as seen in Acts 13:15, where Paul preached at Antioch.

Even as early Christians participated in temple and synagogue worship, they also began meeting on the first day of the week, the Lord's Day, to engage in Christian worship. This act was a fusion of synagogue worship and the experience of the upper room. At the center of vocabulary and form was Jesus Christ. All elements of worship centered around God's actions in Jesus' life, death, and resurrection, and the community celebrated those actions.

In New Testament worship, the laity has clearly been called to service. First Peter 2:9-10 reads, "But you are a chosen race, a royal priesthood, a holy nation, God's own people, in order that you may proclaim the mighty acts of him who called you out of darkness into his marvelous light. . . . once you had not received mercy, but now you have received mercy."

While we know very little about the specifics of Christian worship in its infancy, we do know from reading Paul's first letter to the Corinthians that the proper use of spiritual gifts by all present in worship was encouraged (1 Corinthians 12:4-26; 14:26,40). In Ephesians 5:18-20, worshipers are directed to ". . . be filled with the Spirit, as you sing psalms and hymns and spiritual songs among yourselves, singing and making melody to the Lord in your hearts, giving thanks to God the Father at all times and for everything in the name of our Lord Jesus Christ."

Thus the Judeo-Christian tradition of worship is not a performance one observes, but a service one performs. The Greek derivation of the word *liturgy* is from two words: *laos,* meaning "people" and *ergon,* meaning "work." Thus our liturgy, which is the form for our worship, becomes the work of the people. Jurgen Moltmann wrote that "worship is *not* the work of the people if all the shaping and expressing is done by one individual or group."

The presence or absence of lay participation in the planning and leading of worship can determine the very nature of the service. The absence of the laity's participation results in a performance by the clergy, while the presence of the laity results in a participatory celebration. The ways in which worshipers participate can range from the verbal and cerebral to the aesthetic and creative. To participate in worship means to develop one's God-given gifts. The singer develops artistic and communication skills; the speaker, written and verbal skills; and the active listener, skills of comprehension and integration. All who participate learn the give-and-take of worshiping in community.

If we embrace the idea of worship as the work of the people, pastors and worship committees must take special care to design and plan services that elicit participation from everyone present. We also need to teach people how to worship. Many people feel that worship should be an oasis in the midst of life's chaos, with nothing but their presence expected of them. They come to church for consolation and comfort, expecting the service to meet their emotional needs. Others come to worship to be entertained, feeling satisfied at the end of the service if they have seen a "good show." Others come to this divine drama as critics, observing the service and offering their critique. The problem with this passive approach to worship is that one cannot be an actor and a critic at the same time. Once we remove ourselves from the acting ranks, we distance ourselves from our principal task as humans—to give glory to God. This is not to minimize the good feelings we may experience during worship, but they are a by-product, and should not be the goal of the worshiper.

The worship committee's primary role is to set the stage for liturgy—for the work of the people. It is to provide an atmosphere where authentic worship can occur and prepare the actors and prompters for their respective tasks.

Chapter 1

Worship Identity and Purpose in Your Church

> The religious church which simply takes care of the people will always understand its worship services as church "events" and stylize them as fixed ceremonies. . . . A communal church which is *of the people* will see itself as the subject of its own gatherings and will form its worship into feasts of its own history with God.
>
> —*Hans-Ruedi Weber*
> *Salty Christians*

Before authentic worship can take place in a given church, the congregation's worship identity must be recognized and understood. An opportune time to reflect on an existing congregation's identity is when a new pastor is called or when the organizational structure is changing. If you are involved in starting a new congregation, study and dialogue about how you will "do" worship together may involve the entire congregation, which will prove to be an exciting and stimulating process.

The worship identity of any congregation is organic. It lives and breathes and is always emerging, looking to the future even as it is rooted in tradition. Phillip Dodson has said that "in worship, we reach out one hand toward the future, while with the other, never letting go of the past, for therein lies the present."

The study of and reflection on the history of your church's worship identity begins with the worship committee. Below are just a few ways to gather information about your worship tradition.

Ask members of the worship committee to invite longtime church members to share memories of past worship experiences. You may wish to create a list of questions that interviewers can ask. These interviews might also be audiotaped for future study. These conversations will be mutually beneficial as the elders reminisce and the committee members are given a glimpse of the past worship life of the church.

If your church has archived worship bulletins, review them as a committee. Compare the bulletins from decade to decade or pastorate to pastorate. Pay particular attention to those parts of worship that have stood the test of time. This exercise will give you a snapshot of worship and music styles used over the years.

Then bring these two processes together by gathering the longtime members together with the worship committee to reminisce about worship services and review worship bulletins. Together, you may wish to construct a worship history time line for worship planners. This exercise can also ease the minds of longtime members about changes in worship style by reminding them of the many ways the service has evolved during their lifetimes.

Send out a questionnaire to former pastoral staff. Possible questions might include: What were the worship values of the congregation during your pastorate? How would you describe the predominant worship style? How did you teach worship skills to the congregation? What innovations did you implement during your tenure? What was your greatest challenge in worship leading?

Interview young adults on the membership roll who, for various reasons, are no longer active in the congregation. Ask what they remember most about their childhood experiences of worship. What was most meaningful? What left you cold? What do you appreciate most about worship services you attend today? Would you be willing to attend our worship service and give us your impression as to how it has changed since you were a child? Conversations of this kind with young adults could generate their renewed interest in the life of the church.

Traditions are getting a "bad rap" these days. It seems

as though everything must be new to be valid. The language of worship (invocation, benediction, offertory, and so on) is being replaced with secular terminology. Theological vocabulary is deleted from sermons in order to be more user-friendly. Musical styles are similar to what people hear on the radio. While all of this can produce relevant worship, there is value in maintaining some traditions. Ritual and language help us to remember that we are not on this journey alone. We are connected to past generations as we worship Jesus Christ, the same yesterday, today, and tomorrow. A wise pastor and worship committee will be attentive to the church's worship traditions. For many worshipers, these are vital to their encounter with God.

The past is prologue—to the present! The next step in discovering the worship identity of the congregation is to take a careful look at the current makeup of the congregation. This task could include the preparation of a worshipers' profile, listing gender, age, racial or ethnic background, educational and life experience, styles of music regularly listened to, and even favorite books, plays, or movies. When one congregation gathered this information, the leaders discovered that what they thought was a predominantly Euro-American congregation had over twenty primary languages represented! This contributed to a major shift in their worship identity. Another congregation learned that 80 percent of its members listened to soft rock on the radio and no one listed classical as a music preference. As a result, the church musicians (who to this point had presented only classical music) began to broaden their musical styles to reflect the congregation's aesthetic sensibilities.

Does the worship identity of your church include persons who are differently abled? If you have persons with a hearing impairment, do you engage an American Sign Language interpreter for your services? Does your worship space comply with Americans with Disabilities Act guidelines? Could persons confined to wheelchairs serve as worship leaders in your service? If you have persons with mental handicaps, do you offer special-education worship experiences?

What is your vision for the future of worship in your church? What will your congregation look like in five years? in ten? If you are in an urban setting, are the demographics of your community changing? If you are in the suburbs, are you noticing more young families with children? If you are in a rural area, are young adults moving away or returning to their roots? If you are experiencing an influx of immigrants, are you prepared to have simultaneous translation in your service? Are you equipped to offer services in languages other than your primary worship language? Your city or county can provide demographic projections that may be helpful as you envision your future as a worshiping community.

Will your future worship service use new forms of technology? If so, how are you preparing your congregation for the change? How will your worship space need to change? How will you provide funding for this technology?

How will your congregation "welcome the stranger"—those who have been marginalized, who have experienced only pain and disappointment in their relationship to the church? How will your church minister to Generation X? to Generation Y? to seniors who are encountering God for the first time?

Studying trends in music and worship styles is another way to plan for the future. Worship and music seminars and conferences are plentiful. Your denominational offices can assist you in finding rich opportunities for education.

Balancing past, present, and future in the design and planning of worship is delicate, indeed. It is important for the leadership of the church to regularly reflect on the church's worship identity. This will insure that what occurs in worship is the work of the whole people of God as they offer their corporate prayers and praises.

A church's worship identity helps determine what the purpose of worship is for the congregation. Which of the following best describes the reason that your congregation comes together each week?

Adoration: Worship is a cultic activity intended for believers. The service is altar centered. Little or no auxiliary activities are included. Everything done in the service points to God.

Education: Worship is a learning activity. The service centers around the proclamation of the Word through the sermon. A call to action or response on the part of the congregation is included.

Evangelism: Worship is centered around sharing the gospel. The service is simple and user-friendly to attract nonbelievers (seekers). An intentional invitation to receive Jesus as Savior is given each week.

Fellowship: Worship centers around the gathered community. Opportunities are given for sharing and small-group prayer. The service is congregation centered.

Spiritual formation: The service is designed so that each word, spoken or sung, will facilitate spiritual growth. The form and flow of the service is therapeutic, offering comfort and consolation. The service is worshiper centered.

Many congregations would list all of the above to describe the purpose of worship in their church. The goals of the worship service can change from week to week as the Holy Spirit dictates, but the general nature of the purpose of your worship will tend to fall into one of these categories.

After recognizing and understanding your worship identity, do you find it compatible with your purpose for worship? If not, how will your purpose need to change to reflect the people who make up your church family? One of the roles of the worship committee is to articulate and interpret the purpose of your worship and to insure that the way in which the congregation worships remains faithful to its always emerging identity.

Chapter 2

The Worship Committee

For just as you have many members in one physical body and those members differ in their functions, so we . . . compose one body in Christ and are all members of one another. Through the grace of God, we have different gifts.

—Romans 12:4-6, Phillips,
The New Testament in Modern English

Selecting the Committee

The size and configuration of your worship committee will be unique to your setting. In some churches, size is determined by the official documents of the congregation; in others, it is flexible, based on the nature and scope of its tasks. The size of the committee should be commensurate with other leadership groups with similar authority. In most cases, a committee of six to nine members is most efficient. The configuration of the committee may also be determined by official church documents or may be the result of an intentional selection process by the church's nominating committee. Sometimes, there may be a representative from the choir, Christian education committee, or diaconate.

Effective worship committees are a form of liturgy reflecting the work of the whole people of God. Committee members come to this work with the enthusiasm of youth and the wisdom of age. They are women and men who reflect the cultural and ethnic demographics of the congregation. Members represent a variety of theological positions, aesthetic preferences, and religious experience, and they express their diverse gifts in the many functions of the committee. In the selection process, it is critical to provide the congregation with a balanced ballot representative of the congregation. A balanced list of candidates gives voice to the people, and this kind of inclusiveness allows for a wide range of perspectives. In churches where issues of worship and musical styles are at the forefront of discussion, it may be tempting to create a committee of "like minds," either to preserve the worship traditions of the congregation or to bring about changes in worship style. This may be a short-term solution, but could prove detrimental over time.

The following questions can be addressed by the nominating body:

1. What spiritual gifts does the candidate possess? How can these gifts be used in the work of the committee?
2. How does the candidate demonstrate a love for, even a passion for, worship?
3. Does the candidate have worship-related talents or gifts that could be nurtured and developed through membership on the committee?
4. What is the candidate's potential for spiritual growth by serving as a member of the committee?

One of the benefits of serving on a committee is the opportunity to develop leadership skills. Clergy delight in the growth that occurs in their members through service as church leaders. This is not only important for adults, but vital for young people in the congregation. My own passion for worship began when, as a high-school sophomore, I represented my peers on the worship committee. I remember what a positive experience it was. The adult members and staff treated me with respect, listened to my opinions, and took me seriously. They trained me in the art of agenda building and minutes taking, of serving on search committees, and in giving me responsibility and holding me accountable for my assigned tasks. They spent time with me, educating me about worship, and even let me plan an entire worship service with other members of the youth group (and it wasn't even Youth Sunday!). My involvement shaped me for professional church leadership in significant ways. If you consider having a youth representative serve on your committee, you may want to appoint an adult member to "team" with the young person and serve as guide and mentor. The adult member spends time with the youth representative, perhaps sharing in an occasional meal, listens to concerns, and mentors the young person in the art of church leadership. These relationships often become central to the spiritual growth of both the adult and youth members.

As ministries evolve, the configuration of the committee may change. We need to be sensitive as the Spirit initiates new ministries through the imagination and creativity of the congregation. For example, one young adult leader felt God's call to form a postservice prayer team. Some congregations have been providing this ministry for many years, but for this church, it was breaking new ground. The church bylaws did not include this kind of ministry as a function of the worship committee, but the committee was sensitive to the Spirit and incorporated it into its work. Being flexible to new ministries and able to let go of ministries that "have had their season" is key to keeping the worship ministry alive and vital.

Committee Leadership

The officers of the committee can be appointed by the church moderator or selected by the committee itself. The *chair* must demonstrate a commitment to the importance of worship in the life of the congregation. The chair is the spiritual leader, and must possess the gifts of wisdom and discernment. This person will most likely serve as the committee's liaison with the primary decision-making body of the congregation, and must be an excellent interpreter and communicator.

As "cheerleader," the chair motivates each member, helping each bring her or his vision and dreams to reality. Encouraging and affirming members from time to time is an important and often overlooked task. Occasional notes, phone calls, or e-mail messages are valued and appreciated! Other tasks include preparing meeting agendas in consultation with clergy, providing opportunities for worship and worship education during the meeting, and chairing the meeting, with an eye to the clock!

In most settings, a *vice chair* will function as chair in the chair's absence, and may be assigned other tasks. In churches with less formal polity, the chair and vice chair may function as "co-facilitators," modeling a team approach to leadership for the committee's work.

The *secretary* keeps the committee roster up-to-date, takes minutes of the meetings, (sending them to members as soon as possible following the meeting), and sends reminders of meetings to members. Regular affirmation and encouragement of those involved in worship ministry is an important part of this role.

In some churches, committee members may have specific responsibilities as *ministry team leaders* or may act as the team leader's *liaison* with the committee. These teams may include the ministry of ushers, greeters, music, flowers and decorations, sound and video, and others. The liaisons' role will be discussed in more detail in chapter 6. Most likely, team members will not be members of the worship committee and may be recruited by the ministry team leader or by the worship committee liaison. The team functions under the direction of the worship committee, communicating through the liaison. This approach to shared ministry empowers people to fulfill their call to the worship ministry in a context of mutual support and accountability. Teamwork demands time, energy, and commitment from each member, but the experience reaps innumerable benefits.

This style of working sets the tone for the design of the committee meeting. When the ongoing work of the committee is accomplished outside the meeting itself, more time can be spent looking at the "big picture," working toward the goals and objectives set by the committee. Meetings also tend to be shorter in length, and members and staff leave feeling that their time was well spent. For more information on conducting productive meetings, see David R. Sawyer's *Work of the Church: Getting the Job Done in Boards and Committees* in this series.

Preparing the Committee for Its Work

Before the worship committee begins its work, several important tasks need to be accomplished.

The committee needs to *understand its purpose in the life of the congregation*. Members can read the official documents of the church to learn the general nature of the committee's work and how it relates to other leadership groups in the church. Another document for review is the church covenant, which could be used as the basis for a devotional time in the initial meeting of the committee. Committee members work more effectively when they are aware of how they function within the larger framework of congregational leadership. Perhaps your church's moderator may wish to be present during the first meeting to explain the documents and answer questions.

Another important task is to *build a covenant together.* Created by the committee, this document determines the ways in which the committee will behave with one another. It also provides a wonderful opportunity to learn about the gifts and skills each member brings to the committee's work.

You may wish to use this simple process. Each member lists his or her gifts and skills that are available to the committee. The lists are circulated, so other members of the committee can reaffirm the gifts or skills with a check mark or add gifts and skills they have recognized in each other. Then, as a group, the committee lists its expectations of others in order for them to succeed as a member of the committee. Following is an example:

I can bring these gifts and skills to the work of the worship committee:

For me to succeed as a member of this committee, I need others to:

One or two people take this information and begin the task of drafting the covenant. Here is an example of a covenant compiled from one committee's lists:

"As the worship committee of First Church, we are faithful church members who utilize our gifts of leadership, organization, experience, communication, creativity, follow through and humor in order to provide an atmosphere for vital and creative worship for our congregation."

"As a committee, we covenant to relate to each other with mutual trust, flexibility, willingness to share ideas, listening ears, tolerance, punctuality, faithfulness, emotional support, respect, efficient meetings and . . . a sense of fun and play!"

When every member of the committee agrees to the covenant, it becomes a testament to the rich and diverse gifts of the members and how the committee will interact with one another. (My gratitude to Bud Carroll, retired Educational Ministries staff member in the ABC/USA, for introducing me to this process in 1979.)

Inevitably there will be conflict among members, and it is important that a *process for conflict resolution* be agreed to before conflict occurs. Seeing conflict as a natural part of the cycle of human relationships aids in strengthening teamwork. There are many written resources to assist committees in determining a process. It may also be helpful to bring in someone with experience in conflict resolution to help the committee determine its own process. Time invested at the beginning of a committee's work will be beneficial when the group wrestles with the difficult and challenging worship issues facing our churches today.

Relating to the Pastoral Staff

Most often, the worship committee will be assigned a staff member to provide administrative assistance for its work. The pastor or minister of worship or music is often the most logical choice for this position. The ways in which the committee relates to its staff leaders are crucial to the effectiveness of its work. The worship committee is responsible for the worship health of the congregation and can take this responsibility seriously by praying for and caring about their staff. As the pastor assumes the prophetic role in proclaiming the Word each week, the committee can pray during the week, as the work of prayer and preparation is done, during the sermon or homily itself, and following the service. Opportunities can be given to staff for spiritual retreat to envision and plan for future worship services. When staff is exhausted, the worship committee can advocate with the pastoral relations committee for time away for spiritual renewal.

The relationship and trust level between the staff member and the chair of the committee is critical. They may meet prior to each committee meeting to review the minutes, prepare the agenda, and enjoy mutual spiritual support. As staff to worship committees for over twenty years, I found these relationships to be central to my own spiritual formation, as well as a way of increasing the effectiveness of the church's worship ministry.

The extent of the worship committee's role defines the parameters of responsibility and accountability with church staff. In some churches, the committee creates policy and provides broad guidance for staff, and staff plans and implements the worship services. In other churches, the committee does the planning and implementing, from recruiting lay leaders to selecting the music for congregational singing to printing the bulletins. What is the division of responsibility in your church? Is this clearly communicated to both staff and committee members?

Relating to Other Leadership Groups in the Church

Worship committees do not work in a vacuum. Perhaps more than any other ministry, worship permeates the entire life of the congregation, for in any kind of service, we offer ourselves up "as a living sacrifice, holy and acceptable to God, which is your spiritual worship" (Romans 12:1). Open communication between the worship committee and other leadership groups in the church is critical. How do your church leadership groups communicate with each other to avoid over programming the congregation? Is a master calendar kept? Who mediates when two leadership groups want the same date or space? What happens when another leadership group in the church wishes to begin a ministry that is actually related to the work of the worship committee? Some churches communicate by holding an annual leadership retreat in two parts, each leadership group meeting individually, and then coming together to share their plans for the coming year. Potential conflicts are resolved, and everyone is aware of what the others are planning. Looking at the big picture may also provide opportunities to combine or cosponsor events. For example, during the Advent season, many groups in the church may wish to sponsor events. The Christian education committee may wish to hold an Advent workshop; the diaconate may wish to sponsor a day for spiritual renewal; the worship committee may wish to host the hanging of the greens; the outreach committee may wish to promote a special emphasis on inviting family and friends; and the women's ministries may wish to host a holiday tea, craft fair, or special meal to raise funds for their ministry. Given that Advent is only four Sundays long, would it not make sense to combine some of these events, working together to achieve everyone's goals? Other events that lend themselves to intercommittee cooperation include Easter sunrise services and breakfasts and renewal weekends for the congregation. The committee will also want to work in tandem with the diaconate when they have ideas for innovative communion services and baptisms.

Finding the right people to serve as members of the

worship committee, giving them tools for effective communication, and relating appropriately to pastoral staff and other leadership groups will serve you well in your work.

Chapter 3

The Work of the Committee

God is here in word and action,
God was here before we came.
All creation sings God's glory;
Let us join and do the same.
God in Christ is our salvation;
Grateful hearts respond with praise,
Living lives of faithful service,
In the fullness of our days.

—*Jane Parker Huber*
Singing in Celebration

What is the purpose of the worship committee in your church? Why does the committee exist? *Mission statements* answer these questions. A mission statement can be as simple as "The worship committee exists to provide an atmosphere for authentic worship, reflective of the whole people of God." The process of developing a mission statement takes time, energy, and engagement on the part of every committee member. It is a process that will help the committee keep its energies centered, take ownership of its work, and remain faithful to its call.

Conflict may arise not only as hot issues are discussed, but also in the way things are done. Standard operating procedures (SOPs) will eliminate wasted energy and confusion. Each function of the committee needs a SOP describing specific tasks; sadly, in most congregations, this document does not exist. This is a somewhat daunting project, but thoughtful and clearly written SOPs will benefit not only the current committee, but future committees as well. SOPs are living documents that can be adapted as ministries evolve, and they are vital to insure that tasks are completed in the most effective and efficient manner. They are also invaluable for providing information about the work of the committee to prospective committee members.

One of the worship committee's important tasks is to set *worship policies.* Your committee may already have a complete set of clear, concise, and up-to-date policies that are reviewed from time to time to insure that they continue to be viable for the changing needs of the congregation. Or you may operate under "we've always done it this way" policies—those verbally handed down from the elders of the church without much thought to their relevance. I remember hearing about a "policy" regarding the attire of choir members (who wore robes each week), stating that women were not to wear jewelry of any kind and were to wear black shoes. Men were to wear white shirts, black ties, and black shoes. Clearly, this policy had not been revised for decades, and it was broken by a majority of choir members (including their director!)

The best policies are simply and clearly stated, to the point, and for the good of the whole congregation. To be effective, they need to be consistently implemented. However, there will be times when making an exception to the policy is the right thing to do. Policies, like standard operating procedures, are living documents, requiring periodic revision to maintain their usefulness to the congregation.

Policies Generally within the Purview of the Worship Committee

Applause

Lengthy and heated discussions about the use of applause in worship have kept worship committees in a quandary for many years. In a few churches, everyone agrees that applause is never to be a part of worship, but for the majority, there are people on all sides of the issue. Because each action in worship reflects the theology and values of the congregation, this policy must be written with these things in mind. Whom are we applauding when we hear the choir sing a rousing anthem? Does your congregation applaud a particularly moving sermon? What are we saying to children when we generally applaud their singing but refrain from applauding one week? Are there other kinds of responses better suited to your worship? Does your church engage in "clap offerings" to God? Do people in your congregation feel that applause destroys the flow of the service, as it would in the middle of a symphony or Shakespearean play? The delicate balance between the freedom of the individual worshiper and responsibility to the congregation must be achieved in accordance with your church's worship values.

Building Use for Weddings, Memorial Services, and Funerals

Some churches rent out their facilities to anyone wishing to hold a wedding, memorial service, or funeral. Others rent the facilities only if a member of the church staff officiates at the service. Others do not rent their facilities, holding these services only for members. The church staff may recommend the policy, based on their theological and pastoral understanding of these important life events.

Crying Babies and Fidgety Children

The worship committee and the Christian education committee may wish to work in tandem to create this policy, as it will reflect the ways in which the congregation values children. It is an important issue for churches, requiring careful consideration. Input from and clear communication with families who have young children is vital. Congregations distracted by babies and young children in worship may wish to have designated "family greeters" each week, who are knowledgeable about the location and leadership of child care during the service and escort the family to the child-care area. This is a wonderful ministry for the elders in the congregation, who can offer a "grandparenting" touch, particularly to families visiting the church for the first time, who may be reticent to leave their children with strangers. Young children can be given "worship grab bags" made of fabric and filled with a children's bulletin, crayons, and other items. Information to help parents prepare their children to worship may also be helpful. These proactive measures let families know that they and their children are welcomed and valued by the congregation.

Whatever policy you adopt, if the ushers are to be involved, discuss it with them and provide training for the appropriate action taken in the appropriate manner.

Disruptive Behavior

From time to time, people may attend worship with the express purpose of disrupting the service. Self-appointed prophets may begin to speak during the sermon; during wartime, protestors may picket during the service; persons with mental illness may act out in inappropriate ways. The ushers need a policy that will give them direction in order to respond appropriately in these situations. (Make sure, though, when "disruptive behavior" is a planned part of the worship service, to clue the ushers in! I remember a service that started with a prophesy from Isaiah, spoken eloquently by a church member who was a professional actor, in Old Testament garb, sitting in the midst of the congregation. The ushers didn't recognize him and ran down the aisle in an effort to remove him from the sanctuary. It certainly added to the drama of the moment!)

Emergencies

Who in your church is responsible for knowing what to do if an emergency occurs during a worship service? Is it the job of the ushers? the trustees? the diaconate?

Who decides if a 911 call is necessary? Is there a list of church members who are licensed medical professionals who can be "on call" one Sunday per month? Does the church insurance policy provide for the protection of volunteer caregivers if your state has not enacted a Good Samaritan law? In most churches, the ushers need clear guidelines in order to take appropriate action.

In the event of fire, earthquake or other natural disasters, do you have a plan? Does your church have disaster supplies? Do the people responsible know where the disaster supplies are? Is the first-aid kit readily available? Who keeps it up-to-date and complete? What is the plan to care for children who are not in the worship space? This policy most likely will be set by the property committee, but the worship committee may wish to give input, since it is at worship when the congregation is most regularly and fully gathered.

Inclusive Language

Many churches continue to struggle with the use of inclusive language in worship. For churches who have fully integrated this into their culture, there may be concern when lay leaders do not use it when speaking or reading the Scripture lesson. For churches moving toward the use of inclusive language, the question of revising standard hymn texts is often raised. Some churches are divided, and the issue needs to be addressed with open communication, respect for differing opinions, and sensitivity. Some churches will always subscribe to traditional language.

This is an area where a policy is very helpful, particularly to worship leaders and those who are coming to lead worship as guests. It also informs committees that revise official church documents and recommend pew Bibles and hymnals to the congregation.

Memorial Gifts

In consultation with the memorial committee or your church's foundation or endowment committee (should one exist), the worship committee may determine the way in which memorial funds designated for worship will be used and how the gift will be acknowledged. The days of putting brass plaques on everything from pianos to drinking fountains appear to be over, and a policy will assist the committee and donor in what is appropriate for your congregation.

Musical Instruments for Teaching and Rehearsal

Musical instruments represent a significant financial investment on the part of the congregation, and it is the worship committee's responsibility to ensure that they are used appropriately. In large urban churches, the demand for rehearsal instruments may be great among professional musicians. Some churches will rent rehearsal space to musicians unrelated to the church, while others will allow only the music staff to practice on the instruments. If the staff is also allowed to teach on the instruments, their students sometimes practice on them as well. Often a small rental fee is charged to offset the cost of utilities and instrument maintenance, and in some cases, students will play for services in exchange for the privilege of rehearsing on the church's instruments. Children of church families who cannot afford an instrument may also be allowed to practice.

Photography

There are times when family members and friends wish to record important events in the lives of their loved ones: baby dedications or baptisms, confirmations, weddings, and children participating in worship. How does your congregation respond to still or video photography during the worship service? Some churches encourage this practice, arguing that it makes coming to the worship service a user-friendly experience. Others forbid any form of photography because they view it as a distraction to worship. Others provide an opportunity to "stage" the event either before or after the actual service or provide a professional quality videotape produced by the church's technology team for purchase.

Worship Leaders

In most worship traditions, lay participation in worship is an important part of the service, and in most churches, no provisions are made for the selection and training of leaders for these important tasks.

What is the criterion for leading worship in your congregation? Must one be a church member in order to read the Scriptures or lead in prayer? Is there a minimum age requirement?

Does your church demonstrate its commitment to the training of children and youth as worship leaders by selecting them to participate as leaders on a regular basis? Who trains people in the art of public Scripture reading and prayer? Is training a requirement for people who will lead in worship? Creating a policy for worship leaders will help the committee clarify its values about the role of lay leadership in the worship service.

Your situation will dictate what policies are needed for your congregation. If worship committees are new to you or you have never created policies before, you may wish to move through this process slowly, perhaps creating a few per year. If you have policies in place, the beginning of a new year is a good time to review and revise them as appropriate.

When the worship committee is working on a given

policy, an invitation to appropriate groups or persons to give input will always be welcomed. It may be helpful to have the committee list all the potential groups and people that would be affected by the policy and actively solicit their suggestions.

Once policies are adopted, they should be published in the church's newsletter, and a notebook should be kept in the church office for referral by the staff and congregation.

It is important for the committee to remember that its role is to *create* policy. The role of church staff is to *implement* policies set by the committee. This basic yet important understanding enables the committee and staff to work effectively as a team.

Evaluating the Effectiveness of the Worship Service

Ask a committee member to time each segment of the worship service with a stopwatch for four to six consecutive weeks. You may wish to categorize the time in components—Scripture readings, music, sermon, announcements, fund-raising pleas, and so forth—or you may wish to divide the service between the spoken word, the sung word, the active word, and the silent word. How we spend our time in worship is a good indication of what is important to our congregation—or is it? Your worship committee and congregation may be surprised by the results of such an exercise.

Ask committee members to gather bulletins from other churches from family members, friends, and colleagues for review by the committee. Compare your bulletin to these for user-friendliness, style, font size, and so forth.

Ask a denominational staff member to attend a worship service and make notes as the service progresses. These folks are in different churches from week to week and are invaluable as interested observers. After the service, take the staff member to lunch and listen—really listen—to what she or he has to say. Make it clear that you want honest feedback in order to improve the way your committee "sets the stage" for worship. When that honest feedback comes, be open to hear what the Spirit is saying through this person.

Invite the congregation to provide feedback about their worship experience. This can be as simple as a bulletin insert with the components of worship listed for comments, or as elaborate as a postservice event with professionally produced evaluations that are interpreted by the producing company. Another way to gather information is to host occasional open forums where people can share their perspectives on the worship service. If the lines of communication are continually open in a congregation, chances are that when conflict does occur (and it will), people will trust that their voices will be heard.

Ask the committee to keep a worship journal for a given time period, reflecting on each week's service. When the period is over, ask the committee to list the strengths of the service and areas that need improvement. Sharing opinions about the strengths and weaknesses of the service may indicate what the goals and objectives for the coming year should be.

Most church staff meetings include a time of debriefing the prior Sunday's service. From time to time, you may wish to ask a staff member to take notes to share with the worship committee.

Goals and Objectives

It is important for the worship committee to periodically determine the direction of its work, in addition to maintaining its ongoing tasks. Setting goals and objectives and meeting them will prove to be stimulating to the committee and beneficial to the worshiping congregation. Goals tell us what we are going to do; objectives tell us how we will do it. In some churches, each board or committee is required to publish its goals and objectives for the year and is held accountable for them by the congregation through annual reports.

Goals and objectives can sometimes be set by taking a "gifts inventory" in your congregation. Are there particular gifts among your members to inspire a new ministry? Is there a dancer in your midst who could start a dance ministry? an actor who could begin a drama troupe? someone who loves to work with flowers? artists who could work with children and youth to create worship bulletin covers?

At the beginning of each year, the committee may wish to meet for an extended period of time to set the stage for its work. An agape meal may well be incorporated into this time to celebrate the emerging community within the committee. This is the time to review the functions of the committee for new members; create the covenant; determine the process for conflict resolution; and review the mission statement, worship policies, and SOPs. It is also a good time to reflect on the form and flow of the current worship service and decide on goals and objectives for the coming year.

One of the most important roles of the worship committee is to advocate for worship education in the church. In order for a congregation to mature in its understanding and experience of worship, continual education must be incorporated into the curriculum of children, youth, and adults. The worship committee may suggest that the Christian education committee host a church school elective series on worship, including the study of the theology of worship in the church's tradition, the history of Christian worship, the style and language of worship, hymnody, and the use of the arts in worship. If your church does not have a qualified teacher for this series, you may wish to ask the professor of worship in a nearby college or seminary.

Calvary Baptist Church in Denver, Colorado, has developed a wonderful book to educate worshipers, *Worship at Calvary.* It guides the reader through a worship service, explaining the "whys and hows" of each part of the service and how they flow together. It also defines worship words such as *invocation, benediction,* and *offertory* and explains the theological significance of the stained glass windows in the sanctuary. A resource of this kind would be helpful to new members, could be used in orientation classes or with children and youth, and could be made available in the pews for visitors.

During orientation classes, new members may also appreciate the opportunity to discuss worship with the pastoral staff or members of the worship committee. Reviewing the worship bulletin to better understand the service is very helpful. This is particularly important as congregations reach out to persons who have had little or no relationship with the church.

The worship bulletin is also an excellent tool for education. From time to time, you may want to include a short explanation of each part of the service in the bulletin.

One of the most exciting things a worship committee can do to educate children and youth is to sponsor a worship arts camp. Activities may include everything from creating bulletin covers to learning about the mysteries of the hymnal, writing poetry, singing in a choir, and learning about and playing the instruments used in your service. Participants learn to speak the Scriptures in public (they love to be videotaped!) and can learn to write prayers. Communion bread can be baked and the table set for a special time of learning about the Lord's Supper, led by the pastor. Campers may even design, plan, and lead the worship service for the following Sunday.

One of the most important functions the worship

committee performs is to be available to the congregation during times of change. Discussions about worship and music style continue to divide churches that do not give intentional thought and prayer to the process of change. The worship committee is the group that hears the concerns of various groups in the church, wrestles with these issues, and interprets the decisions made to the congregation. When changes are to be made, the committee acts as a pastoral presence for the congregation. If the committee has done its homework to prepare people and is seen as open and available to all segments of the congregation, the process of change can be a more positive experience for everyone.

For the worship committee to be effective in its leadership, it is important to provide time for the group to worship together and share the concerns and celebrations of their lives. The committee then becomes more than a task-oriented group, but rather, a microcosm of the body of Christ, providing a place for mutual spiritual support.

Chapter 4

The Work of the People: Worship Design and Planning

> When we plan worship
> I help my friends to praise, pray
> and say thanks to God.
>
> —*Japanese Senru Poem*
> *written by Amy, a ten-year-old worship planner*

Worship is the work of the people as we participate in praise, prayer, proclamation, and remembrance. This truth has alternately been valued and ignored through the centuries. Since the early 1960s, we have experienced a "liturgical revival"—a season for an increase in the participation of laity in the design, planning, and leading of worship. It is a time for artists and writers, dancers and musicians, weavers and potters, actors and poets. It is a time for all voices to be heard as we resonate as one in praise to God, our Creator, Redeemer, and Sustainer.

The idea of lay people planning worship is not new. It is, however, frightening to both laity and clergy. Who will assume the prophetic role in selecting the theme and scriptural foundation for the service? Who will plan what? How will the components of worship be coordinated? Who will make the final decision when there are conflicting opinions as to what should be done? What role does the pastor or preacher play in the design and planning of worship? Who is ultimately accountable to insure that all the details are in place each week?

In some churches, the pastor plans the content and flow of the service from beginning to end. He or she knows the intent and direction and desired result of the service. The pastor either has selected Scriptures, or used the lectionary, and selects all songs for congregational singing. He or she presides over the service.

At the other end of the spectrum, some churches rely heavily on the worship committee to plan services. Each member may be responsible for planning a series of worship services, sometimes based on seasons in the Christian year. The worship committee member selects a worship-planning team from the congregation to select the theme, Scriptures, and preachers (which may or may not be the pastor). The team plans and implements each part of the service, becoming the prophetic voice for the congregation.

Some churches combine the best of these two approaches, with clergy and laity working together to create an atmosphere for vital and creative worship. The prophetic role may be performed by the clergy at some points and laity at others. The committee and staff study the Scriptures together to develop a shared vision for the worship service. Some groups continue to share insights with each other through the week through e-mail, fax, or telephone.

Often worship committees appoint worship-planning teams to do this work. The team should be representative of the congregation, including seniors, boomers, members of generation X, and teenagers or children. In my experience with worship-planning teams, the most effective teams included a teen or child as a full member. They offer profound wisdom and fresh insights as they view worship through their unique perspective. If your congregation is ethnically diverse, the planning team should reflect this richness.

The work of the worship-planning team can begin with a period of silent, spoken, and perhaps sung prayer. Each time the team gathers, they begin by giving space for the Spirit to speak, to be still before God to hear what God wants to do in worship, and to pray for each other's needs. Sometimes this period may include modeling different forms of worship, including Taize, liturgical morning or evening prayer, or centering prayer.

The next step in worship planning is to develop the theme for the service or series of services. What will your

focus be? What does God want to teach your congregation through these services? If your church uses the
lectionary, the theme will emerge from the appointed
scriptures. If you do not use the lectionary, the pastor,
preacher, or the team may select scriptural passages. The
group then exegetes the passage. Each member of the
team shares his or her perspectives about how the passage is relevant to the life of the congregation.

After the "big picture" is in place, it is time to design
and plan the components of the service. Each member
of the team may plan the same component of worship
for a series of Sundays. For example, one person may be
responsible for planning the way in which the congregation is called to worship, varying its style each week. The
team member gathers people from the congregation to
determine the content (Scripture, published or original
poetry or prose) and form (monologue, dialogue, unison,
or a combination), decides where the call will come from
(pulpit, balcony, rear of the worship space, aisle, or aisle
while processing), and determines if the call will include
music (choral, solo, handbells, or other instruments).
The team then recruits leaders for each week and gives
them their script and rehearsal times well in advance of
the service.

The same process can be followed for the proclamation of the Scriptures (read, acted, sung, danced, unison
or one voice, choral reading) and the leading of the
prayers of the people. While this process may at times
seem disjointed, it ensures that within a given series of

services, worshipers experience a variety of ways in which the Word is communicated. It also keeps the team members focused on similar tasks.

When the components are prepared, the planning team meets again to hear the reports of the members. The team reviews the flow of the service, to make sure that all components are faithful to its theme. They also look at the transitions in the service, to ensure that the atmosphere is in place for a full range of responses appropriate to the service. For example, an uplifting element in worship will be more uplifting when what precedes or follows it is contrasting in mood or style.

The team members then implement the planning by scheduling and rehearsing the participants. Following the service, the team can write notes of appreciation to the participants.

Seasons in the Christian year provide a rich framework for worship planning. The four Sundays in Advent may be a good place to begin if your church has not included laity in worship planning before. The planners may suggest a theme and weekly themes that could be incorporated into all of the activities of the congregation during this season. If your church uses the lectionary, the framework will already be in place. There are many supplementary resources to the lectionary that enhance scriptural themes through music, prayers, litanies, poetry, and art. Banners, dance, and drama can add to the creativity in this season. The traditional themes of hope, peace, joy, and love can be incorporated as well. What a rich time for the people to plan worship!

Other seasons well suited to worship-planning teams are Christmas–Epiphany, Lent–Easter, and Eastertide–Pentecost. Asking volunteer teams to plan more than seven weeks will be difficult, since the enthusiasm and commitment required to produce quality worship can wane.

Worship-planning teams meet not only to plan worship but to learn about worship. Time can be dedicated to worship education at each meeting, led by a member of the pastoral staff, a team member, or a professor of worship at a nearby seminary. The history of worship in your tradition can be reviewed, worship terms defined and explained, a comparative study between pulpit- and altar-centered worship can be done, and current worship styles can be explored.

Just imagine if you organized four worship teams per year, involving five to seven people on each team. In ten years, over two hundred members of your congregation will have a solid understanding of worship in your tradition from their participation as planners and leaders.

One of the major benefits of using worship-planning teams is that you profit from the collective thinking of the team in selecting participants to lead the service. One person planning worship can never know the extent of the gifts, talents, and skills demonstrated in the congregation. Working together, the team can share its knowledge of potential leaders in worship and often can identify persons who have never been considered as leaders. I have witnessed the benefits that worship leading brings to persons who are asked to participate. It is a wonderful way to enrich spiritual growth and renewal.

The process of learning to be a leader in worship helps develop people in ways that produce benefits beyond the worship service. Learning to read the Scriptures in public develops public-speaking skills and self-confidence. Leading the congregation in prayer enhances spiritual growth as the leader takes on the priestly role of bringing the prayers and petitions of the people to God. Time spent in preparation and reflection sensitizes the leader to the needs of the congregation. The leader begins to think beyond the "I" to the "we" of corporate prayer. Training for this holy time is necessary, to avoid subjective rambling or inclusion of personal agendas. The role of lay worship leaders also extends past their time at the pulpit. Regardless of where they are seated during the service, they are looked to as models and teachers. Their actions, reactions, and attentiveness give the congregation behavioral clues.

Training worship leaders is particularly fulfilling when working with children and youth. It is essential that their participation include more than the traditional "Youth" or "Children's Sunday." Planners must include children and youth on a regular basis and communicate this commitment to the Christian education committee.

Children and youth need quality training and adequate rehearsal in order to give their best as worship leaders.

They will respond well to seeing themselves read or pray on videotape. They will know how important they are when they are coached by the best teachers, writers, actors, and public speakers in the congregation. Their self-confidence will grow, they will develop new skills, and they will educate their peers about what it means to worship God. When preparing materials for children, it is helpful to produce a large-print copy of the Scripture lesson. When the passage is entered into the computer, create spaces to indicate where the reader is to pause. Then highlight the words that are to be stressed. Ask the child to practice every day with a parent or older sibling, or call the child and listen to the passage over the phone. The 5 1/2"-by-8 1/2" reading copy can then be inserted into a Bible or folder.

Chapter 5

The Lively Arts in Worship

There are ideas, insights and experiences which only sound can communicate, others only communicated by movement, others which only color and line can capture. This is why the arts offer insight into God, each other, and ourselves which can be offered in no other way.

—*Judith Rock*
Full Circle

Music enables us to worship God with our minds *and* our hearts. This combination of the cognitive and affective is what makes music a unique medium in our worship experience. Music prepares the soil of the heart to receive the seed of the gospel. It is an attention getter, a persuader, and a catalyst in breaking down resistance to the message of God. In the Scriptures, God commanded us to "sing unto the Lord," "to make a joyful noise," to "sing psalms, hymns and spiritual songs." Making music for God's pleasure is not optional. It is the way of the Christian to offer musical praise and prayer. Music occupies a large part of the worship service in most churches today. When you time the components in your worship service, you may discover that half of your service is worship through music.

In some churches, music ministry is given high priority. Larger churches employ a full-time director or minister of music. Smaller churches may hire a part-time director, who often may be a music teacher from a local school or have other employment. In churches where congregational singing is given a large block of time in the service, a praise and worship team coordinator may be hired. In each of these cases, the person may or may not be the primary keyboardist for the congregation.

The interaction between music staff and worship committee will be unique to each congregation. Some committees give complete creative freedom to the music staff, asking only for a report at the end of each year. Others may require more frequent reporting, and still others may wish to approve everything the music staff does, including the selection of music. It is important that worship committee members and music staff both understand the lines of responsibility and accountability. In most cases, the music staff administratively reports to the senior pastor. The committee functions as an advisory and policy-making body.

Many times staff members feel as if they have many

bosses. Members of the worship committee, by virtue of their elected role, may feel that they are empowered to supervise the activities of the music staff and, in some cases, the pastor. It is important when forming a worship committee or hiring new staff that clear lines of account-ability be drawn. Most often, appraising the work of staff lies with the personnel committee or pastoral relations committee. The worship committee may from time to time wish to communicate affirmations and concerns to the appropriate body, and personnel or pastoral relations committees may wish to elicit information from the worship committee during periods of staff appraisal.

When it is time to hire new music staff, what is the worship committee's role? Some committees will serve as the search committee, and others will be represented on the committee by their chair. The worship committee may then meet with candidates and make its recommen-dation to the final decision-making body. It is important that the committee be involved in this process in the manner appropriate for the congregation.

Some music staff members may be contributors to the worship committee, attending meetings, leading church music education sessions, and resourcing the committee as needed. Some may serve as the primary staff person to the work of the committee, assisting the chair in developing meeting agendas and providing administra-tive support.

Whatever your polity is, it is important that the lines of communication be open, with all parties involved.

Everyone should understand the appropriate places for input and discussion. This is particularly important today, when discussions of music style are at the forefront of church life.

Has your church experienced tension about musical styles in worship? Do you have heated discussions about the virtues of traditional, contemporary, or blended worship? Do most discussions about worship occur in the parking lot after services or meetings? Your church may be experiencing a major shift in its worship identity. During these times, it is important that the worship committee have a conflict-resolution process in place. Members of the congregation need to know where to go with their concerns about worship and music style.

When new styles of music are introduced into the worship service, persons who are uncomfortable will often complain to each other or to the pastor. Their complaints may be related more to the *way* in which the new style was introduced, rather than to the style itself. It is a rare congregation that can sight-read new hymns and songs with proficiency. The church's musicians can teach new music in various settings—in church school classes, small groups, Bible studies, and social events. The song can also be played as a prelude or offertory to introduce the tune to the congregation. A soloist can sing it the week before the congregation sings it for the first time. The story of how the song was written can be included in the bulletin. Then, when the new hymn or song is finally sung in the worship service, most people will sing it with a level of comfort.

The worship committee is instrumental (no pun intended!) when major purchases are needed. When a church requires a new hymnal or collection of praise and worship songs, the committee can either become the "congregational singing search committee" or select a committee representative of the congregation. (Remember to include a youth representative in this process, since this book will be used for many years.) The committee may also be responsible for raising funds for the project, if funds have not been allocated in the church's budget.

Whoever facilitates the search will benefit by moving through the process slowly. In most congregations worshiping in the free tradition, the hymnal or songbook is used as much or more than the Bible in worship. The language and musical style of this resource reflect the congregation's theology and values. For some churches, the selection process is simple. Each time the denomination revises its hymnal, the church purchases copies. If your denomination does not publish a hymnal, an intentional search process will be helpful.

The hymnal search committee begins by reviewing several hymnals or collections, comparing them in a variety of ways for theological content, language, number of songs in a variety of musical styles, sufficient number of songs in a variety of content categories, font size, number and range of indices, and supplementary worship resources. Make sure that the hymnal fits into your pew racks or that you can make the necessary modifications. This initial process requires a few months of review and appraisal, and the entire process can take up to one year to complete. It is critical that the congregation be given the opportunity for input. You may wish to create a space where the congregation can review the books, providing a notebook for comments. This is a wonderful time to educate people about the ways in which hymnals can enhance public worship and private devotion. When you order the books, be sure to order extras to offer to church families and individuals for use at home. When the new hymnal is selected and purchased, a festival of singing with a time of dedication will be a true celebration of the work of the people!

The Hymn Society of America has good resources to help congregations in the selection of hymnals. If your congregation primarily uses contemporary praise and worship music, *Worship Leader* magazine will be helpful to you in selecting collections of songs.

When other purchases are needed, such as choir robes, handbells, Kodaly or Orff instruments, organs, pianos, or keyboards, similar processes will apply. Gathering information and input from the congregation will assure that these investments will be valuable to the life of your congregation for years to come.

Other lively arts used in worship include drama (in its many forms) and dance. Most churches are not in a position to hire professionals to coordinate these

ministries, so talented volunteers are recruited to provide leadership. Given the rigors of developing good
groups of dancers and actors, it may be helpful to have
a member of the worship committee act as a liaison with
the leaders. The liaison may function administratively,
informing and reminding people of rehearsals, coordi-
nating costumes and props, and assisting with the setting
and cleaning up of rehearsal space. The worship committee can serve as the primary advocate for these ministries, helping congregations to understand and feel
comfortable with what may be new avenues of worship
expression.

Chapter 6

The Worship Budget

For where your treasure is, there your heart will
be also.

—Matthew 6:21

Finding adequate financial resources for ministry is
always a challenge. Limited funds must be appropriately
shared by all of the church's ministries, based on the
values of the congregation. The worship committee's
budget is a "snapshot" of the importance of worship in
the life of the congregation.

Building a worship budget is a good way for the committee to appraise the value of the varied tasks that make
up the worship ministry. After your committee has written
standard operating procedures for each part of its work, it
is good to review these for clues about where funds
might be appropriately spent. In addition to funding the

ongoing work of the committee, an item for new or emerging ministries may be helpful. This fund, however small, will encourage leaders who have a vision for new ministry.

A periodic review of the budget is important, other than at "budget building time," when there is pressure to meet deadlines imposed by budget committees. Some churches hold listening sessions, where members of the congregation are invited to meet with members of the worship committee to share their dreams and visions for the worship ministry of the church. These sessions will often produce wish lists of musical instruments, techno-logical equipment, and other items that enhance or ex-pand a worship ministry. Other churches gather information through written surveys completed after the worship service on Sunday mornings. Churches may also invite designated visitors to the worship service to solicit their impressions about how the service reflects the church's worship values. All of these tools are helpful to the committee in discerning the most effective ways to use its portion of the church budget.

In years when giving is static, developing a budget can be an exercise in the wringing of hands as commit-tees try to decide which items can be reduced or com-pletely eliminated. During these times, it is more important than ever to see the budget through a different lens—to study what is vital to the worship health of the congregation. If cuts to the budget need to be made, this may be the time to review the goals and objectives set by the committee at the beginning of the year. The committee should have input into any reductions mandated by a decrease in giving.

Imagine entering a church, to be greeted by immaculately groomed ushers with white rose boutonnieres pinned to their lapels. An usher directs you to your seat and hands you a bulletin printed on expensive paper. The front of the pulpit boasts an enormous bouquet of exquisite flowers. The large choir enters the sanctuary in beautiful robes. They begin to sing in dulcet tones, leading the congregation in the great hymns of the faith, accompanied by pipe organ and string orchestra. Solos and anthems are offered, the Scripture lessons are thoroughly prepared and thoughtfully read, and beautiful prayers are prayed. The pastor, regal in a black robe, preaches an eloquent and stirring sermon. Following the service, an elegant coffee hour is hosted for members and visitors. The values of this congregation are clearly demonstrated in the worship service. It is obvious that formal traditional worship is considered of prime importance, and adequate funding is provided for such an experience.

Now look at your worship service. What is demonstrated to be important? How does your service reflect the financial values of your congregation? Are you using choir anthems from the 1940s? Does the drummer in your praise band have to use empty plastic containers and pans? Does your organ squeak and whine because it has not been maintained? Have you run out of bulbs for your overhead projector? Is the piano out of tune? Is the sound system antiquated? Are your pew Bibles tattered and torn? It is the task of the worship committee to pay attention to the worship needs of the church and address those needs in the budget.

Items to consider when developing a worship budget include:

- Staff compensation: salary, retirement plan, medical insurance
- Guest director, organist, keyboardist
- vacation, continuing education, and sick leave for regular staff
- Audiovisual technology: maintenance, repair, purchase
- Drama and dance: scripts, costumes, sets, props
- Music library: for choirs or praise teams
- Music copyright license fees: annual and one-time use
- Music maintenance: organ and piano tuning and repair, electronic instrument and handbell repair, choir robe cleaning
- Flowers and decorations: weekly and seasonal, banners, flags, candles
- Hospitality supplies: ushers' and greeters' name tags, visitor brochures
- Special music: musicians for festival services and concerts
- New or emerging ministries fund
- Worship bulletin covers: stock, seasonal, or custom designed

Your budget reflects the importance of worship in your congregation. It is an effective communication tool for the congregation, because they can see where their giving is allocated.

When it is time to submit your budget to the church's budget committee, present it in annotated form. Many times, budget committees are handed a set of figures without any explanation, which makes reducing those figures rather simple. State your case to the budget committee. Better yet, ask that a representative from the worship committee be present to verbally present the budget. (In many churches, this is common practice.) You may also want to attach your worship ministry "wish list" to the budget.

The reality of church budgets is that they are not adequate for visionary ministry. When special opportunities present themselves (choir tours, large purchases, and so forth), other means of funding may be necessary. When other sources of revenue are needed, the worship committee needs to understand the church's fund-raising policy. If you need approval by another leadership group in the church, present your case in a clearly written fashion, complete with a description of the situation (the organ has died), an action plan (how you will raise the funds to bring the organ back to life by serving 1,000 spaghetti dinners) and the benefit to the congregation (we won't have to sing a cappella anymore!). The deciding group will see that you have a real need, have the action plan to back it up, and can produce positive results for the congregation. If your case is presented clearly and enthusiastically, it will be difficult to deny your request. If your church operates only through the church budget, ask the committee to increase your budget when you need to spend over your allocation. It's just like Jesus said, ask, and you shall receive. If you are turned down the first time, don't be discouraged. Ask again in six months, and keep asking until you have what you need to be faithful to God's call for the worship life of your church.

Chapter 7

The Infrastructure of the Worship Ministry

> Now there are varieties of gifts, but the same Spirit;
> and there are varieties of services, but the same
> Lord; and there are varieties of activities, but it is the
> same God who activates all of them in everyone.
>
> —*1 Corinthians 12:4-6*

The work of the worship committee is a ministry of service. In order to create an atmosphere where vital worship can occur, planning and preparation are essential. Often these functions provide some of the most creative opportunities in the life of the church. There is also a plethora of perfunctory and mundane tasks that need to be completed, giving church members of all ages the opportunity to participate.

One way to organize the work of the worship committee

is through ministry teams. Ministry teams imply that
something meaningful and germane to spiritual growth
can occur in the context of teamwork, rather than just
serving a functional purpose. Ministry teams can be
coordinated by either a member of the team, who becomes its team leader, or a member of the worship
committee, who becomes its liaison. The number and
purpose of ministry teams will be unique to any given
congregation. However, the following are common to
most worship committees.

The Ministry of Hospitality

Today's church is called to be a safe haven for people
living in a turbulent society. After the stresses of the
week, it is good to arrive for worship and be greeted by
a friendly hello and warm smile. This "first contact" of
corporate worship is a crucial moment. In some
churches, the ushers may be a stand-alone organization,
but in a majority of churches, it is the function of the
worship committee to provide a liaison to support and
affirm their efforts. The *ushers ministry team* leader or
worship committee liaison recruits ushers who demonstrate the gift of hospitality, schedules the ushering team,
develops training opportunities for new ushers, provides
continuing education for experienced ushers, and com-
municates ushers' concerns to the committee. Liaisons
can encourage the ushers through creative acts of appreciation throughout the year. *The Work of the Usher*, by

Alvin D. Johnson, in this series is a good resource for this ministry of hospitality.

Some churches provide two opportunities for worshipers to be greeted, using a *greeting ministry team* in the parking lot or at the outer entrance of the worship space. This is an excellent opportunity for intergenerational ministry, allowing children, youth, and adults in a variety of configurations to exercise their gifts of hospitality. The worship committee can provide a liaison for the greeters, whose tasks are similar to those of the ushers' liaison. If you decide to include children and youth in the greeting ministry team, it is important that they feel comfortable in their role. Training events can be a fun time of intergenerational connection as adults and children role-play several situations that could occur while greeting worshipers.

The Ministry of Prayerful Preparation

Preparing for worship through prayer is vitally important. Many churches now have pre- and postservice prayer teams to provide spiritual undergirding and support for the worship service. The preservice team invokes the presence and power of the Holy Spirit and prays for each person who will lead in worship. Sometimes prayer teams continue to pray throughout the service, timing the sequence of their prayers to the order of worship. The postservice team prays with and for persons who have been moved by the service in a special way or who have need for spiritual counsel or healing.

A worship committee liaison can coordinate this ministry by recruiting persons who demonstrate the gifts of
prayer and healing, scheduling the team and providing
training opportunities. The liaison also affirms members
of the prayer team through regular acts of appreciation
for their ministry.

Enhancing the Physical Space

Worship requires all of our senses. We see the beauty
of stained glass, wood, or marble—or the simplicity of
modern architecture— and we watch as the Word is acted
or danced. We speak and sing our praise and prayer.
We hear the Word of God spoken and sung, and we
listen in communal silence for God to speak. We smell
the fragrance of fresh flowers and candles. We touch
each other in greeting and fellowship. The aesthetic
possibilities for each congregation are many, and it is
the worship committee's task to enhance the physical
environment for worship. The committee may appoint
a liaison to coordinate the flowers that adorn the
gathering and worship spaces, offering church members a schedule of available dates to donate flowers.
The liaison may also develop a team of artists to design
and create decorations for special seasons in the church
year and provide opportunities for the whole congregation to participate, as in the hanging of the greens
during the Advent season. In some churches, national
flags are sometimes used in processions to visually

enhance prayers for the world or to decorate the space. The liaison coordinates their use, care, and storage.

The use of fine art has been woefully ignored in Protestant worship. We have lost the mystical truths found in sign and symbol. This important ministry can be resurrected by your worship committee. A member of the committee can be responsible for creating alternating art exhibits in the gathering space of the church, where local artists can show their work. Children, youth, and adults can also develop their gifts through art seminars and workshops. Art teachers in the congregation are a wonderful resource for curating these exhibits to show the work at its best. Fine art can also be used in the creation of bulletin covers and as an enhancement to Scripture readings, anthems, and sermons through slides and video.

The importance of preparing the worship space is often overlooked. Pew racks need to be free of clutter; Bibles, hymnals, and songbooks straightened; attendance, visitor, and offering materials replaced; offering containers placed in the appropriate location; and candles lit when appropriate. In large churches, these tasks may be assigned to a paid staff member, but in smaller churches it is often the worship committee that coordinates this ministry of service.

Using Technology to Enhance Worship

We live in an age of technology that offers a wealth of possibilities for worship enhancement. These opportunities come with the responsibility to ensure that technology will enhance worship and not distract the congregation. Most churches have used sound systems for years, developing the gifts of a sound ministry team. Many times the sound operators are not given any information about what to expect during a service, resulting in poor sound reinforcement. A liaison from the worship committee can communicate the worship plans to the sound operators and coordinate rehearsals and sound checks for the worship leaders. A simple form assigning microphones to the worship leaders for every part of the service will give needed cues to the sound operators. The liaison can also schedule operators and backup operators, coordinate the sale of audio or videotapes following the service, and regularly affirm the team for its work.

Using newer forms of technology in worship can be exciting and somewhat scary! If the worship committee's vision is to incorporate technology into the service, it is important that this be done thoughtfully and slowly, gathering input from the congregation. Installing a projection screen over the baptistry without any warning has been the cause for more than one church split! Once the congregation is on board and equipment purchased, the committee can provide a liaison to recruit and train operators for stage lighting, overhead, data, and video projection. The liaison schedules the team and supports and encourages it in its ministry. These "invisible" tasks are vital, and many times are overlooked in the planning and preparation for worship. They deserve the investment of time, energy, funding, and affirmation on the part of the committee.

Supporting the Lively Arts

The ministries of music, drama, and dance give people of all ages the opportunity to offer their gifts to God in worship. They require an active support system in order to function with ease. Does your church choir wear robes? Is there someone to coordinate robe assignments, use, and care? Does your church have a music library? Who catalogs and cares for the music? Is there an orchestra? Who sets up and takes down music stands and lights? Do you have a graded choir program? Who assists with transportation, arranges snack times, and offers help with "crowd control?"

Do you use drama or dance? Who is responsible for the creation and maintenance of costumes and props? Who builds and decorates the stage? The worship committee can work through a ministry team to provide support to the drama and dance troupe leaders.

The Ministry of Lay Worship Leading

Lay participation in worship is highly valued in a vast majority of churches today. Training laypersons to become leaders in worship is an important part of the work of the worship committee. It has been said that "it's a curse to rehearse," yet what appears to be seamless improvisation in worship is almost always the result of careful thought and planning. A liaison from the worship committee can work with worship leaders, training, scheduling, and affirming them. Some churches select a group of people to lead worship for a specific period of time and provide training for effective speech communication, including the use of videotape for personal and group critique. Teaching people to write and deliver congregational prayers can also be done at this time. Speech teachers, communication consultants, actors, retired ministers, or other qualified persons can be solicited to lead the training.

Each week the liaison can meet with worship leaders, rehearse with the sound system operating, and give instruction about when, where, and how the leaders will move from place to place during the service. The leaders can then meet with the pastoral staff for prayer prior to the service. Lay leaders can be encouraged to support one another by praying for their peers as they lead in worship.

The Sacraments/Ordinances in Worship

The service of the Lord's Supper and baptism are important elements of corporate worship. In most denominations worshiping in the free tradition, the diaconate is responsible for the physical arrangements for these experiences. If the worship committee has creative plans to alter the way in which communion or baptism will be done, it is important to work collectively with the diaconate and the pastoral staff to avoid unnecessary conflict. Occasions when creative communion experiences may be effective include Worldwide Communion Sunday (where baskets of ethnic breads may be brought to the table by persons from a variety of backgrounds), Thanksgiving (with seasonal decorations on the communion table symbolizing the bounty of God's goodness), and Maundy Thursday (where people may come to the table and be seated in groups of twelve for a more intimate experience) or an agape meal may be served.

Printed Worship Materials

In most churches, bulletins are given to each worshiper as a guide to the service. If you use a bulletin, how does it reflect the values of your congregation? To visitors, opening the bulletin is like receiving a road map. If one is an experienced worshiper, her or his eyes will be drawn to the "particulars" of the service. What songs will be sung by the congregation? Do I know them? Is there a children's story? Does the church use drama or dance in its worship? If visitors are new to church life, they may want clear instructions (rubrics) to help them maneuver through the service. When do I stand? When do I sit? What books do I use, and when do I use them?

Some churches make an intentional effort to create a user-friendly bulletin that may include all of the Scripture texts or the page numbers in the pew Bibles, the texts of any presented music, copies of the songs for congregational singing, and an outline of the sermon. Devotional texts for meditation prior to worship are included, as is information about the music for the service. The worshiper needs only to refer to the bulletin (which could be several pages in length) to fully participate in the service. What does this "all-inclusive" bulletin say about the place of Bibles, hymnals, and supplementary books in the life of the congregation? Should participating in worship be this effortless?

Other churches do not use bulletins at all, claiming that they distract people from worship. The service format is made available to the worship leaders, but to the worshipers, the service seems spontaneous. Only song texts are projected onto screens, and worship leaders verbally guide the people throughout the service. What does this say about the value of music in the congregation, when people are singing wholly by ear?

Most churches purchase stock bulletins from their denominational offices or local Christian bookstore. The format is skeletal in nature and includes basic information about the service. The worship committee may wish to vary the size and format of the bulletin for special seasons in the Christian year. Bulletins created by artists in the congregation, new paper sizes, and colors will grasp the attention of worshipers.

From time to time, it is good for the worship committee to review the look and format of the bulletin. A task force could be created for this purpose, comparing your church's bulletin to others with a similar worship style. The group then can bring any recommendations for change to the worship committee.

Visitor Information

What kind of information does your church distribute to visitors? Is it distributed during the worship service or available in the pews? Sometimes the production of this information is under the purview of the worship committee. The information could be in brochure form, including a welcome from the pastor, highlights of the ministries of the church, and a summary of its beliefs. A card for visitors to register their attendance may also be included.

How does your church register the attendance of its regular worshipers? Is this important information for your church leaders? Many churches invite worshipers to register, using either a card or book in the pew. Cards will sometimes include space for prayer requests or messages to church staff. The worship committee often has responsibility for periodically reviewing how this information is gathered.

Publicizing Worship Events

How does your church publicize its worship schedule? Do you have an ad in your local telephone book? When was it last reviewed? Do you have a standing ad in your local newspaper? Is it attractive to visitors? Do you have a message on your telephone that includes the times of your services? A member of the worship committee can create effective ads and messages by working with a church member who has advertising or public relations experience.

Advertising special services and events or concerts is very important. Press releases and ads can be created for newspapers, television, and radio stations. If you are offering child care or free admission or parking, include this information. Don't be afraid to spread the word that your church has planned something special for the community. This is an excellent evangelistic tool.

The support of the infrastructure of the worship ministry is crucial to the effectiveness of worship in your church. All of these tasks are important, meaningful acts of worship in and of themselves. Committee members who take on these tasks need regular encouragement and affirmation.